The Splendour of St Paul's

BY E. T. FLOYD EWIN, MVO, OBE, MA

Registrar and Receiver of St Paul's

JARROLD COLOUR PUBLICATIONS
NORWICH

FOREWORD BY THE DEAN OF ST PAUL'S

No one who comes to St Paul's wants to be bored with details. We all hope to learn something, enough to help us to appreciate the Cathedral and we expect to go away with firm impressions and visual memories. This book will lead all our visitors to achieve this end. The account of the past and the present is short and interesting and the pictures are superb. This production can be used in two ways. It can be taken as a handbook and guide, as people walk about the Cathedral and it can also be used as a vivid record, and reminder.

St Paul's cannot be taken in by one exploration. Each time we enter, it says something new to us. I hope all those who come to the Cathedral will try not to hurry. Look up and look about you. Try to get the 'feel' of the building. Take it in, with expansive glances, like gulps of air entering your lungs. There is a grand and impressive sweep about this building. Let the eye follow it and enjoy it. Occasionally stop and examine some point of detail, as you would do in a picture and then go back to the wider vision.

Before you leave, sit down with this book in your hand and re-live the experience through which you have just passed. Meditate quietly upon it, with joy and with gratitude, that you have been privileged to enter upon it. As you gaze at some photograph, suddenly look up and see the original before you. Remember, at all times, that the beauty in the design, and the history behind the walls point not to themselves but to the glory of God and the service of man.

And then, at home, especially if you come from abroad, this book will bring you back across land and sea, into St Paul's once more. You will walk about it again, see it, and almost touch its pillars. As you turn the pages, you will momentarily be within its walls. We welcome you and rejoice in your fellowship.

MARTIN SULLIVAN
Dean of St Paul's

CONTENTS

85306 404 0
© 1973 *Jarrold and Sons Ltd, Norwich.*
Printed and published in Great Britain by Jarrold and Sons Ltd, Norwich. 173

The publishers are grateful to Associated Newspapers Group Ltd for the supply of the picture reproduced on the endpapers; and to Aerofilms Ltd for the aerial view reproduced on page 48.

One of the most famous photographs of the last war (reproduced in this book) shows St Paul's illuminated by the fire that swept the City of London after the devastating bombing raid on the night of 29 December 1940. The great dome stands intact above the burning buildings that surround it, a symbol of enduring hope, and of resurrection.

There is a story which tells of Sir Christopher Wren marking out the ground-plan of the new cathedral amidst the rubble of Old St Paul's destroyed in the Great Fire of 1666. He sent a workman to fetch a large piece of stone to mark the centre of the dome at the crossing of the transepts with the nave and choir. The heat-damaged stone that the workman brought carried one word, *Resurgam* – 'I shall rise again.'

OLD ST PAUL'S

There may have been a church on this site as early as the fourth century, but the first recorded account dates from 604 when the diocese of London was created by St Augustine, Mellitus installed as Bishop, and a church dedicated to St Paul sponsored by Ethelbert, King of Kent. After the death of King Ethelbert the church was destroyed in the pagan reaction which swept through southern England. After about forty years Christianity returned to London and from *c.* 675 to 693 Erkenwald was Bishop of London. He re-founded the cathedral and was later canonised. Miraculous cures were claimed for those who touched his carriage, and his shrine was a popular venue for pilgrims. However, his popularity was never enough to change the cathedral's dedication, and it is remarkable in England that London's Cathedral has always been St Paul's (for there are few churches earlier than the eighteenth century that take the Apostle's name).

The Saxon church was destroyed by fire in 1087, and the Norman bishop of London was vigorous in starting a new and magnificent cathedral. St Paul's was still only half completed in 1135 when a fire broke out on London Bridge and swept north-eastward through the city damaging the cathedral. Building continued for another 200 years, the Norman style yielding to Transitional and then to Early English. The massive Norman columns were replaced in the choir as clustered pillars. The size of the building was enormous, by the beginning of the fourteenth century it was 690 feet long and the spire 520 feet high. The nave had twelve bays as did the chancel, while the transepts each had five bays. The two towers at the west end were placed outside the aisles. At the east end was a very beautiful and elaborate rose-window similar to the one in Westminster Abbey but larger.

This great building dominated London from the top of the slight hill on which it was built. It was particularly impressive when seen from Southwark, on the opposite bank of the river. Its extensive precincts were enclosed by a high wall and rather than walk round the perimeter of this, people on errands found that, by entering the precincts by one of the six gates and walking through the nave or transepts of the cathedral, they were provided with a short-cut. This traffic soon developed so that people carrying merchandise passed through the building, perhaps resting for a moment in the shady coolness of the nave. The profanation increased when those with goods to sell brought them into St Paul's and even set up stalls. Advertisements were fixed to pillars and merchants found the broad aisles a convenient place to meet and do business. With the fashionable, the central aisle of the nave became a popular after-dinner promenade; in 1628 John Earle (later Bishop of Salisbury) wrote bitterly of 'Paule's Walk': 'The visitants are all men without exceptions, but principal inhabitants are stale knights and captains out of servis, men with long rapiers and breeches, who after all turn merchant here, and trafficke for news. Some make it a preface to dinner and travel for a stomach, but thriftier men make it their ordinary, and board here very cheap. Of all places it is least troubled by hobgoblins, for if a ghost would walk here he could not.' It is interesting to remember that Falstaff engaged Bardolph in Paul's Walk in *King Henry IV*. At this time the desecration of the cathedral was at its height, but the decline had begun centuries before. In 1561 the spire had been struck by lightning, and the resultant fire, after destroying the spire, spread to the roof. The damage was severe, the foundations of the tower being shaken by the fall of the spire. Although repairs were speedily made (the spire was never rebuilt although several designs were submitted) these were badly done and were instrumental in causing the subsequent deterioration of the fabric.

The passions roused by the Reformation hardly left St Paul's unscathed. Men were burnt to death for their faith on scaffolds erected near the great west door. Rich ornaments were confiscated and melted down and effigies removed, later to be restored when Mary came to the throne. The gatherings in front of the open-air pulpit, Paul's Cross, would be stormy when the preacher enthused over the Papist doctrine. This famous pulpit had attracted the finest preachers in the country; sermons usually lasted for at least two hours and often the monarch and the Lord Mayor were there to hear them. Paul's Cross was situated on the north side of the churchyard. Today a tall pillar stands near the place where the old pulpit used to stand.

In James I's reign the dilapidation of the cathedral was so serious that the King was forced to act on the many petitions he received on the subject. A commission was set up, and one of its members was the Royal Surveyor, Inigo Jones. The survey concluded that if the cathedral was to be restored to its former glory about £22,500 needed to be spent on it. This colossal sum allowed for the re-erection of the steeple. A public subscription was opened and enough money collected initially for work to start on restoration to the designs of Inigo Jones. Jones was the leading architect of his day. His enthusiasm for the doctrine of classicism as expounded by Palladio left him entirely unsympathetic to the Gothic style of Old St Paul's. Firstly he concentrated on making the old structure safe. The decayed stonework was taken out and the building refaced with dazzling white ashlar. Classical windows were introduced while pilasters superseded the medieval buttresses of the nave and transepts. Jones' main effort was in the great Roman portico erected over the west front. There were two main reasons for this work, which was sponsored by King Charles himself. The western end of the cathedral was unimposing – possibly it had been left incomplete by the medieval builders; secondly, by constructing the gigantic portico, it was hoped that some of the secular transactions that had previously been carried out in Paul's Walk would be conducted more properly beneath the portico outside the church. John Webb, the pupil of Inigo Jones, wrote of the portico as bringing 'the envy of all christendom upon our nation for a piece of Architecture not to be paralleled in these last Ages of the World', while Wren himself judged it 'an entire and excellent Piece' adding that 'it occasion'd fair Contributions' – i.e. it stimulated the public to give funds for further restorations.

But the Civil War intervened before further work could be undertaken. The Roundheads wrought havoc on the furnishings of the

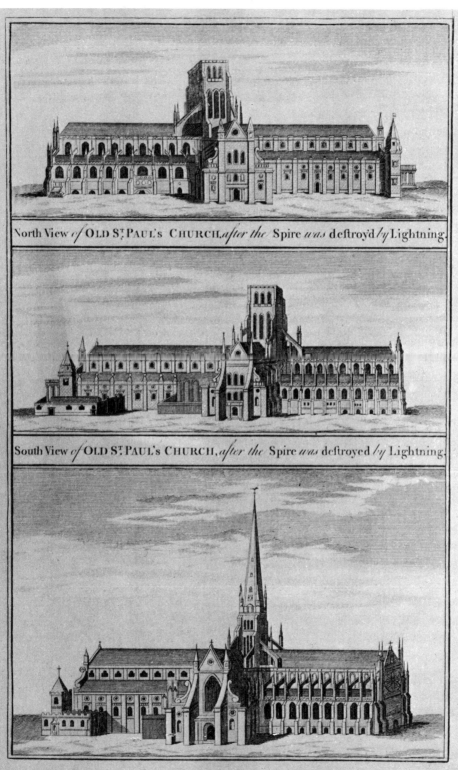

North View *of* OLD St. PAUL's CHURCH, *after the* Spire *was* deftroyd *by* Lightning.

South View *of* OLD St. PAUL's CHURCH, *after the* Spire *was* deftroyed *by* Lightning.

South View *of* OLD St. PAUL'S, *when the* Spire *was* ftanding.

An old print illustrating the grandeur of Old St Paul's.

cathedral, even using the nave as a stable. It is said that Cromwell contemplated selling St Paul's to the Jews to use as a synagogue but this may be apocryphal. Certainly the great church suffered severely during the period of the Commonwealth, even Inigo Jones's great portico being converted into shops and lodging-houses. By the time of the Restoration the cathedral was in a dangerous condition and a Royal Commission was set up in 1663 to inspect the fabric. Urgent repairs were carried out immediately, at a cost of £3,586 in the three years before the Great Fire. Many of the houses that huddled up the wall of St Paul's were demolished and scaffolding erected round the tower preparatory to rebuilding the steeple. In 1665 the plague came and as the epidemic spread terror through the city forcing thousands to flee to the country, work on the cathedral ceased.

CHRISTOPHER WREN: THE EARLY YEARS

In 1665, when the epidemic of bubonic plague in London was at its height, Christopher Wren was in France mainly occupied in studying the great French buildings of the Renaissance. Wren was the gifted son of an eminent churchman, the Dean of Windsor, and was born in 1632. His uncle, Matthew Wren, was even more famous as Bishop of Ely. Christopher Wren was educated at Westminster School and went on to Oxford in 1649 with a considerable reputation as an up-and-coming mathematician. In fact the young Wren was a prodigy, yet, unlike most prodigies, he lived up to the promise of his youth in his later years. He astonished his elders at Oxford by inventing countless instruments which ranged from a gadget enabling one to write in the dark to 'a Way of Imbroidery for Bed Hangings cheap and fair'.

Wren continued at Oxford until 1657: by this time he was a Fellow of All Souls and a respected figure in the field of science. In 1657, at the age of twenty-five, he was appointed Professor of Astronomy at Gresham College, London. Here he gave a weekly lecture to 'some of the politer genii of our Age', as he called them in his inaugural address: an audience of learned scientists, not untutored undergraduates. John Evelyn, the famous diarist, frequently attended Wren's lectures and became a great friend, calling him 'that miracle of a Youth'. The Royal Society, founded in 1661, came into being as a direct result of these weekly meetings. Shortly afterwards Wren became Savilian Professor of Astronomy at Oxford, a position he held until 1673 when the pressure of his architectural work forced him to resign the chair. Wren's early inventions show that he had a firm interest in the techniques of building. His papers, 'Building Forts in the Sea' and 'Inventions for making and fortifying Havens' have a particular relevance, since in 1661 or 1662, the King asked Wren to survey the fortifications of Tangier Harbour and promised him the position of Surveyor-General when the present senile holder of that post, Sir John Denham, should die. About the same time Wren was designing Pembroke College Chapel, Cambridge, his first building, and the Sheldonian Theatre at Oxford, his earliest masterpiece.

Wren made his only visit abroad with but one of his works completed – the Chapel of Pembroke College. It was certainly an opportune time to spend in France especially as his health had always been delicate and 97,000 were to die in London of the plague in 1664–65 – 8,297 in the worst week.

On his return to England Wren enthusiastically brought out his new ideas for the restoration of St Paul's. He had been one of the advisers to the Royal Commission since 1663

The impressive vista down the Gothic nave of Old St Paul's.

and his new proposals horrified the conservative colleagues on his committee. The feature they were most opposed to was the imposing dome that he proposed to erect over the crossing, eliminating the great central tower; it would be the first of its kind in England. Unable to convince his colleagues, Wren submitted his report to the Commission over his name only. No action was taken over this controversial scheme yet Wren was not discouraged when asked to survey the fabric again for the Royal Commission early in 1666. This too advocated a cupola over the crossing, and warned that the building was in a dangerous condition, the pillars leaning outwards under the immense weight of the roof, and the tower tilting as one of its great columns settled on insecure foundations. This proposal was inferior to the later 'Rejected Design', its worst feature being the great pineapple, 68 feet high, that was to go on top of the graceful lantern above the cupola. Above the pineapple there was to be a ball and cross.

With Wren the Commission went to the cathedral to consider these proposals on 27 August 1666. After much argument it was agreed that an estimate should be prepared on the basis of Wren's designs. Just five days later the Great Fire began in a baker's shop in Pudding Lane and swept through the City of London destroying Old St Paul's *en route*.

AFTER THE FIRE – THE THREE DESIGNS

Evelyn describes the scene of devastation after the fire had swept through St Paul's: 'At my returne I was infinitely concern'd to find that goodly Church St Paules now a sad ruine, & that beautifull Portico (for structure comparable to any in Europ, as not long before repaird by the late King) now rent in pieces, flakes of vast stone split in sunder, & nothing remaining intire but the Inscription in yhe Architrave which shewing by whom it was built, had not one letter of it defac'd: which I could not but take notice of: It was astonishing to see what imense stones the heate had in a manner Calcin'd, so as all the ornaments, Columns, freezes, Capitels & projectures of massie Portland stone flew off, even to the very roofe, where a Sheete of Leade covering no lesse than 6 akers by measure, being totaly mealted, the ruines of the Vaulted roofe, falling brake into St Faithes, which being filled with the magazines of bookes, belonging to the Stationers, & carried thither for safety, they were all consumed burning for a weeke following: It is also observable, that the lead over the Altar at the East end was untouch'd; and among the divers monuments, the body of one Bishop, remain'd intire. Thus lay in ashes that most venerable Church, one of the antientist Pieces of early Piety in the Christian World, beside neere 100 more.'

Immediately after the fire Wren was more concerned with completely redesigning the City of London than the ruins of Old St Paul's. The fire had provided an opportunity for broad new streets of stone or brick houses to replace the squalid alleys, narrow streets and jerry-built timbered dwellings of seventeenth-century London. Within the City walls 436 acres were devastated: 13,200 houses, 87 parish churches and the halls of 44 Livery Companies were lost. Wren presented his survey directly to the King within a fortnight of the fire breaking out. His two main broad, straight thoroughfares through the City converged on St Paul's Cathedral, which he envisaged to be a natural focal point for his street plan. Unhappily the necessity of providing accommodation for the City's homeless proved irreconcilable with a revolutionary concept in town-planning.

Wren's first survey of the ruins of the old cathedral was made in February 1667. The Dean, Dr William Sancroft, was anxious to make some part of the building safe so that he could again hold services there. Wren at first agreed that it would be possible to make safe the western end of the nave, and expert masons endorsed this opinion. Work on the restoration did not start for another year however, and in the meantime Wren inspected the ruin again and wrote to the Dean, for now he was less confident about the safety of the fabric. Shortly afterwards Sancroft wrote to Wren at Oxford, 'What you whispered in my ear at your last coming hither is now come to pass. Our Work at the west end of St Paul's is fallen about our ears.' Perhaps the architect was not altogether displeased about this news, for with a patched-up usable church people might have viewed complete rebuilding less enthusiastically. The Royal Commissioners were now left with no alternative but to instruct Wren to demolish the remains of the great Gothic cathedral still standing, salvaging as much of the original fabric as possible. They also had to decide on the form and function of the new church, which if possible should enhance the prestige both of the nation and of the Reformed Church. Since the Reformation the sermon had played a vital role in the church service and in medieval cathedrals only a small proportion of the large congregation had been able to hear the preacher. Furthermore the congregation was now taking part in the service and wished to see clearly all that was going on – in pre-Reformation days the ritual of Communion took place in the Sanctuary, very remote from the congregation. This change of function radically affected Wren's first design for St Paul's, submitted in 1669. Another factor which influenced this plan was financial; he wrote to Sancroft, 'I think it is silver upon which the foundation of any work must be first laid' and though the Dean replied that if the design be splendid enough, then donors would be encouraged to give funds, Wren's New Model Design is less spectacular, though certainly no less controversial than the Great Model Design of 1673, which was also rejected. The main feature of this first proposal was a rectangular nave with the congregation seated looking inwards, most of them in galleries. A domed vestibule would provide an assembly and the church proper was entered up a flight of steps. The width of the nave was narrow to allow Arcades below the galleries, *outside the walls of the church*, where people could meet and promenade: in effect the colonnades were to replace 'Paule's Walk'.

The Surveyor-General's new plan did not suit the public or the clergy (Wren had been made Surveyor-General in 1669 on the death of Sir John Denham). It was generally felt that the design was not grandiose enough to be appropriate to a prosperous capital city; and so Wren in 1673 set to work again and produced a masterpiece – the Great Model Design.

By 1673 Parliament had voted that for each chaldron of coal unloaded at the Port of London the St Paul's restoration fund should receive $4\frac{1}{2}$d – or £5,000 per annum – a modest yet dependable source of income. Perhaps encouraged by this Wren presented the King and the Commissioners with the idea of a spectacular new cathedral dominated by a massive yet graceful dome. Another smaller dome surmounted a western extension which served as a vestibule, entered through a splendidly imposing portico. The main part

Old St Paul's – the west end as remodelled by Inigo Jones 1631-41.

of the church is in the form of a cross with arms of equal length connected by quarter circles like a Greek cross. The wonderful beauty of this design is best appreciated by seeing the great wooden model made by Wren that is in the Trophy Room.

Although the King approved the plan Wren suffered acute disappointment when it was rejected by the Commission. There were two reasons – firstly, its shape did not permit the choir to be built before the rest of the cathedral; secondly, the circular arrangement

This print is from the architect's drawings and is dated 1702.

of the stalls was disliked. Wren must have been terribly discouraged when the clergy turned this new masterpiece down, even the knighthood conferred on him by King Charles two days before could have held little consolation.

Nevertheless he proceeded to produce yet another design, a compromise in which the traditional long cruciform plan was used so that the choir could be completed before the rest of the building and surmounted by an odd-looking mixture of dome, lantern and spire. The King gave his assent to this design on seeing that all the features that the clergy had insisted on were incorporated. Fortunately he agreed that the architect could make working alterations to the plan if necessary. As the earliest biography of Sir Christopher Wren quaintly records: '. . . the King was pleased to allow him the liberty in the Prosecution of his Work to make some variations, rather ornamental than essential, as from Time to Time he should see proper; and to leave the whole to his Management'. Sir Christopher made the fullest use of this in the building of the new St Paul's.

THE REBUILDING

Work on demolishing the ruins of Old St Paul's had begun long before the final design of the new cathedral had been approved. The task was considerable, some of the walls and pillars standing 200 feet high. Men with pick-axes had achieved great feats in razing lesser parts of the fabric, but hand tools were useless against these monsters. To tackle them Wren introduced two new ideas. The first and most spectacular was gunpowder, and in the first instance he supervised this work himself (having asked advice from a gunner at the Tower), allowing an eighteen-pound charge to be placed well inside the masonry, and ignited with a fuse. The result was most successful. A great column was reduced to rubble in seconds, which would have taken weeks or months to pull down by hand. Unfortunately a later use of gunpowder, administered by one of Wren's subordinates, was less successful. He failed to hide the charge deep enough with the result that the shops and houses around the precincts suffered a bombardment. Luckily no one was injured, though a large stone flew through a casement and into a room where two seamstresses were working. Pressure by local residents made Sir Christopher abandon this form of demolition, though some of the great towers still stood. His next idea was to make a great battering-ram from a mast of a ship forty feet long. At its end was a steel spike and fifteen men each side operated it. After the first day's arduous work with it aiming at the base of an enormous piece of towering masonry, no result was apparent, and its operators were sceptical of its effect. Wren encouraged them to persist, however, and soon on the next day a crack appeared, followed by the disintegration of the section. This ancient method was employed against all the high standing fabric remaining, with eventual success, though the west end of the nave and Inigo Jones's great portico were not demolished until 1687. One of the major problems facing the architect were the heaps of spoil that were spread haphazardly over the site. This made surveying for the new foundations a difficult and tedious task, for the sight lines had to be taken round the obstacles. A large part of the stone was retained as being of use for the new cathedral; some was sold as rubble. Melted lead from the roof was salvaged, re-refined, and stored in preparation for the roof of the new building.

At last, on 21 June 1675, a start could be made on the foundations. A snag was found almost immediately. The lines of the new

St Paul's differed slightly from those of the old and at the north-eastern corner the seam of pot earth on which the foundations rested was unable to support the immense weight. In Roman times a potter had dug a pit into the seam at this point. Because of this a shaft had to be dug down to the underlying gravel upon the basic London clay underneath. Then a masonry pier was built up through the gravel beds to take the weight of this foundation.

The organisation necessary to build a structure as large and as complex as this would be daunting today: in the late seventeenth century it was even more difficult. Armies of craftsmen had been recruited, and the architect had to be certain of their skill. Supplies of building-stone came from many different quarries, but the chief difficulty here arose from obtaining the beautiful white Portland stone which was used for the exterior surfaces. The larger blocks of stone had to be winched up from the river to the site, a process which could take days. Sir Christopher was also deeply involved in the raising of finances for the rebuilding, as well as in constructing fifty new City Churches and many other buildings such as the Chelsea Hospital (he wanted to use one of Inigo Jones's lantern towers from the west end of Old St Paul's in this building but the Commissioners refused him permission). The architect contributed generously from his own pocket as well as suggesting many new ideas on methods of fund-raising.

In accordance with the wishes of the clergy work started at the eastern end with the construction of the choir. Yet Wren always visualised the building as an integral whole – no part could be considered in isolation without reference to the rest of the cathedral. Already he had radically altered the concept of St Paul's as expressed in the Warrant Design and the foundations were laid accordingly.

The outline of the planned cupola was inflated into a full-blooded Renaissance dome which, as in the Great Model Design, would dominate both the interior of the building and the sky-line of the City. Wren also did away with external evidence of the aisles, for their low outline on the outside of the building would have spoilt the purity of the line that he intended. Instead false walls were built up to hide the clerestory windows and the flying buttresses (about the only medieval feature voluntarily borrowed by Wren for this building). These 'sham walls' also serve to support the nave wall (and the dome too) by strengthening the buttresses with their counter-weight.

In these early years of building the work involved was staggering, even though it was being concentrated on the choir. Below ground-level bricklayers and masons were occupied with the ingenious vaulting of the crypt as well as with the deep foundations. Perhaps it was not surprising, then, that by 1682 with the walls of the choir only a little higher than the roofs of surrounding houses, querulous voices were being raised to ask where the enormous amount of money given to St Paul's was spent (the amount raised at this time was £10,000 to £14,000 per annum).

The great project was always at the mercy of political factors and in the final years of Charles II's reign these badly influenced the amount of money available for the new cathedral. By his support of Catholics and Nonconformists he lost the confidence of the wealthy merchants of the City of London. The three severe winters of 1678–79, 1680–81 and 1683–84 also delayed progress, the last being the famous occasion when a fair was held on the frozen surface of the River Thames for six weeks or more. King Charles II died in February 1685: for four years he had ruled without Parliament as a despot supported by the Tory gentry. This presented a new crisis for the new cathedral, since in 1687 the Act of Parliament which granted St Paul's revenue from the import of coal would expire. If this Act were not renewed all work on the building would certainly cease. Fortunately King James summoned Parliament on coming to the throne and one of the first measures passed was an increase in the income to the cathedral from £5,000 to £19,000 per annum. Shortly afterwards Parliament was again adjourned and did not meet again for another four years. Although a Roman Catholic, the factor which was eventually to lead to his deposition, King James always took an interest in the rebuilding of St Paul's. His enemies asserted that this was because he wished to see it as a Roman Catholic cathedral, but his reign was short: anti-Catholic feeling in the country was so strong that on his Queen presenting him with a son and heir, William of Orange was persuaded to make a successful attempt on the throne with his wife Mary, daughter of Charles II.

Meanwhile the Surveyor-General had been altering the original concept of the nave and west end of the cathedral. He had never been satisfied with the Gothicised nave of the Warrant Design, which compromised the dramatic effect of the dome. As Jane Lang says in her authoritative *Rebuilding of St Paul's*: 'The nave lost its Gothic self-assertiveness, subdued into a prelude leading to the centre of interest, the great dome.' Wren also reintroduced the idea of the west end as a spacious vestibule with a Morning Prayer Chapel (now St Dunstan's Chapel), a chamber for the Consistory Court (the Chapel of St Michael and St George) on either side, and with the Library and other apartments above. These enlargements made the existing plans for the exterior of the west front inappropriate, so the architects gave the portico two storeys,

A print dated 1747 shows the west façade with the railings and statue of Queen Anne.

each with paired columns in the Corinthian order. These alterations – substantially more than the 'variations rather ornamental than essential' that Sir Christopher was unofficially allowed – were approved.

Although the new monarch showed little interest in the cathedral his indifference was not shared by his wife. Queen Mary, interested in architecture like her Stuart forebears, asked to see how the building was progressing soon after her arrival in London, and was shown round by Sir Christopher. Her admiration for the work is reflected in her sending him venison from Windsor for the annual Accounts' Day dinner. The French Wars, with the ensuing naval blockade, interrupted stone supplies and also drastically reduced funds since few colliers came to London to unload. Eventually this crisis was overcome when

held in place by a complex arrangement of timber spars sprung from the brick cone. The ageing Sir Christopher inspected the work each Saturday morning, being hauled to the upper part of the building in a basket. At last all was complete – the last stone of the lantern was laid at a simple ceremony in October 1708 by Sir Christopher's son, and soon afterwards the scaffolding was taken away to reveal Wren's masterwork in all its glory.

Even with the outside finished and the architect now seventy-six years of age, Sir Christopher's activity at St Paul's was not at an end. By this time taste in architecture was towards the more flamboyant Baroque, and the new Dean and his colleagues came into dispute with the architect over his plan for the decoration of the interior. The Dean and his Commissioners wanted a dome painted with scenes of St Paul's life. They eventually got their own way, and commissioned Sir James Thornhill to do the work. It is undoubtedly

brilliantly done, but in monochrome the effect is far less spectacular than mosaics would have been. Upsets like this led Wren to take less and less part in the final stages of the building, until in 1718 Court intrigue deprived him of the post of Surveyor-General to the Crown originally given him for his lifetime. After this, for the remaining five years of his life, he was content to come to the cathedral as an ordinary visitor, sitting quietly in the great building which had occupied so much of his lifetime and contemplating, perhaps, the various changes from his original plan. He died peacefully on 25 February 1723 at the great age of ninety-one. The Latin inscription on his monument in the crypt has been translated: 'Below is laid the builder of this Church and City, Christopher Wren, who lived above ninety years, not for himself but for the public good. Reader if you seek his monument, look about you. He died 25 February 1723 in the 91st year of his age.'

The face of London is changing constantly and one day, perhaps, we shall be able to see St Paul's from the river in all its glory, unencumbered by the polyglot collection of warehouses and offices that hide its southern aspect today. Nevertheless, the dome can never be hidden, and it makes a fine landmark for river trippers even as far away as Westminster.

It is interesting to contemplate the immense effort and organization that enabled the great blocks of stone to be brought from the Portland quarries to the site of St Paul's. When Inigo Jones was rebuilding the western facade of the old cathedral contemporary chroniclers record with awe the transhipment of a particularly large slab of Portland stone comparing it with the building of Stonehenge. It took about thirty men some six days to haul it from the quay up the hill to the cathedral. All sorts of accidents could befall the stone en route from Portland; shipwrecks occurred and at least one shipload was delayed by pirates.

The dome as it appears from the northern tower of the west front.

Opposite: *This is the wonderful vista of St Paul's that strikes the visitor as he enters the cathedral and moves from the aisles to the nave.* Below, left: *St Dunstan's Chapel is in the north aisle of the cathedral.* Below, right: *This colossal monument is dedicated to the Duke of Wellington.*

Above: *A spectacular view of the underside of the dome from the crossing. The monochrome paintings by Sir James Thornhill depict incidents in the life of St Paul.* Left: *A Flower Festival in the cathedral.* Opposite: *The choir is embellished by the exquisite woodcarvings of Grinling Gibbons. The diarist John Evelyn discovered the talent of this young craftsman and recommended him to Wren.*

The modern baldachino incorporating Wren's first conception of the High Altar.

Above: *The High Altar is separated from the choir aisles by intricately worked wrought-iron gates, the work of the Frenchman, Jean Tijou.* Below: *The apse, behind the High Altar, contains the Jesus or American Memorial Chapel. It is a monument to the 28,000 Americans who, based in Britain, lost their lives in the Second World War.* Opposite: *Looking west from the High Altar.*

Left: *More exquisite ironwork separates the Lady Chapel from the south aisle. The statue of the Virgin and Child behind the altar was a part of the great Victorian reredos.* Below: *The beautiful Chapel of the Order of the British Empire in the crypt was dedicated in 1960. The Order is awarded to men and women who have done outstanding work in the service of their country at home or overseas.* Opposite: *The tomb of Nelson in the crypt.*

Above: *The crossing from the Whispering Gallery.* Opposite: The Light of the World *by Holman Hunt.*

THE
OF THE
LIGHT
WORLD

BEHOLD I STAND AT THE DOOR AND KNOCK IF ANY MAN
HEAR MY VOICE AND OPEN THE DOOR I WILL COME
IN TO HIM AND WILL SVP WITH HIM AND HE WITH ME.

The Chapel of St Michael and St George at the western end of the south aisle.

Above: *The chapel in the north-west corner of the cathedral is dedicated to All Souls and to the memory of Lord Kitchener – the famous Commander-in-Chief who died in 1916. Below left: This memorial door is close to the north-west entrance. Below right: The tomb of General Gordon – hero of Khartoum – in the south aisle.*

Opposite: *The font, which stands in the north transept, was the work of Francis Bird who also carved the statues on the west front of the cathedral. It was completed in 1727 and cost £350. This transept was severely damaged by a bomb which crashed through roof and floor to explode below in the crypt. Below: The inner dome (of brick) is decorated with eight monochrome frescoes illustrating the life of St Paul. They were painted by Sir James Thornhill between 1715–18.*

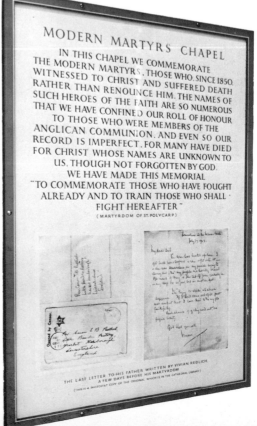

Opposite page, top: *A detail of the carving at the top of the Bishop's Throne.* Below: *An example of the exquisite carving of the choir stalls – the work of Grinling Gibbons.* Above and opposite: *At the eastern end of the north choir aisle is the Chapel of Modern Martyrs which honours Anglican martyrs since 1850. The marble crucifix was part of the high altar reredos destroyed by enemy action in 1940.*

MODERN MARTYRS CHAPEL

IN THIS CHAPEL WE COMMEMORATE
THE MODERN MARTYRS, THOSE WHO, SINCE 1850,
WITNESSED TO CHRIST AND SUFFERED DEATH
RATHER THAN RENOUNCE HIM. THE NAMES OF
SUCH HEROES OF THE FAITH ARE SO NUMEROUS
THAT WE HAVE CONFINED OUR ROLL OF HONOUR
TO THOSE WHO WERE MEMBERS OF THE
ANGLICAN COMMUNION. AND EVEN SO OUR
RECORD IS IMPERFECT. FOR MANY HAVE DIED
FOR CHRIST WHOSE NAMES ARE UNKNOWN TO
US, THOUGH NOT FORGOTTEN BY GOD.
WE HAVE MADE THIS MEMORIAL
"TO COMMEMORATE THOSE WHO HAVE FOUGHT
ALREADY AND TO TRAIN THOSE WHO SHALL
FIGHT HEREAFTER"
(MARTYRDOM OF ST. POLYCARP)

THE LAST LETTER TO HIS FATHER WRITTEN BY VIVIAN REDLICH
A FEW DAYS BEFORE HIS MARTYRDOM
(THIS IS A PHOTOSTAT COPY OF THE ORIGINAL WHICH IS IN THE CATHEDRAL LIBRARY)

The macabre effigy of John Donne was one of the few monuments to survive the Great Fire. Donne was Dean of St Paul's from 1621 until his death ten years later. He posed dressed in his shroud.

These gates divide the south choir aisle from the south transept. They show the outstanding craftsmanship of Jean Tijou, a Frenchman who was a genius with wrought iron.

The backs of the choir stalls are carved just as intricately as the fronts. Again the carvers worked under the direction of Grinling Gibbons.

REMEMBER BEFORE GOD
SIR ALEXANDER FLEMING F·R·S·
DISCOVERER OF PENICILLIN
WHOSE ASHES REST
BENEATH THIS PLAQUE
BORN 6 AUGUST 1881
DIED 11 MARCH 1955

The great dimensions of the crypt with its serried ranks of pillars and beautiful vaulting make a visit there unforgettable. Amongst the many interesting memorial tablets is the one to the discoverer of penicillin, Alexander Fleming. The crypt has two chapels; the small one shown below is dedicated to St Christopher.

LAWRENCE
OF
ARABIA

JOSEPH SIMPSON
K·B·E K·P·M
1909 - 1968
POLICEMAN

1931 CONSTABLE METROPOLITAN
CHIEF CONSTABLE NORTHUMBERLAND AND SURREY
COMMISSIONER OF POLICE OF THE METROPOLIS 1958-1968

A selection of monuments in the crypt appear on these two pages. Note especially this Tudor monument from Old St Paul's (badly scarred by the Great Fire) and Sir Christopher Wren's simple tombstone. The awesome funeral carriage took the Duke of Wellington to his burial here.

The great monument to Admiral Nelson (left) is situated in the south transept, and from here stairs give access to the Whispering Gallery (left, below), over 100 feet above the floor of the nave. Whispered words can be heard clearly on the opposite side of the Gallery, 111 feet away. The Library (opposite page, top), not generally shown to the public, can also be reached from here. Designed by Wren, it houses a priceless collection of books and manuscripts. The bells of St Paul's came through the generosity of the City of London in 1878. Great Paul is the largest and weighs nearly seventeen tons.

The geometrical staircase in the south-west tower is one of the wonders of St Paul's. It was designed by Wren and constructed by one of his master-masons, William Kempster, and is embellished by delicate wrought-iron work by Jean Tijou. It is not usually shown to the public. Opposite: *The grandeur of St Paul's, as seen from the western gallery.*

The old Victorian buildings that used to crowd up to the walls of St Paul's have gone now – either destroyed by bombs in 1940 or by demolition men more recently. Instead the cathedral is surrounded by modern office blocks of steel, glass and concrete. Although architects contrive to make these upturned matchboxes look different from one another on the ground, their individuality is totally lost when they are viewed from above. St Paul's however, retains all of its massive dignity even from this viewpoint, and Wren could never have dreamt of men looking at the building from this angle. The aerial view shows the cathedral as it is – the spiritual centre of a hard and angular commercial world, an enduring symbol of the living Christ.